D1487316

All About
Yellowstone

Lew Freedman

BLUE RIVER PRESS

Indianapolis, Indiana

Published by Blue River Press
Indianapolis, Indiana
www.brpressbooks.com

Distributed by Cardinal Publishers Group
A Tom Doherty Company, Inc.
www.cardinalpub.com

ISBN: 978-1-68157-102-7

Cover Design: David Miles
Book Design: Dave Reed
Cover Artist: Robert Perrish
Editor: Dani McCormick
Illustrator: Amber Calderon

Printed in the United States of America

7 6 5 4 3 2 1   18 19 20 21 22 23 24

Contents

All About
Yellowstone

Preface

Yellowstone National Park was created by the United States Congress as the world's first National Park on March 1, 1872.

The reason the government chose to take this pioneering action was to protect this special place from people who might want to change it by opening businesses and building offices and houses. Yellowstone contains boiling hot springs, waterfalls, forests, mountains, lakes, rivers, and wildlife. Those in charge believed this beautiful section of the United States should be set aside to be preserved for all Americans to enjoy and experience.

That meant people could not build houses, build regular stores to start businesses, or hunt the animals for food inside the Park.

The goal from the beginning was to protect the wilderness inside the Park so future generations would be able to visit and admire it.

The way things worked out, Yellowstone National Park was located mostly in the state of Wyoming, but partially in Montana and Idaho, too. Yellowstone is a very big place, so big that at 2.2 million acres, it is about the same size as Rhode Island and Delaware combined.

Making Yellowstone a park turned out to be a very smart plan. From the beginning, Americans from all over were curious to see what made Yellowstone a unique place. They traveled for hundreds or thousands of miles by train, and later by car, to see geysers like the famous Old Faithful, which erupts at regular time periods and impresses audiences with spurts of hot water. They wanted to see grizzly bears, black bears, bison herds, elk, mule deer, and antelope as they ran around in their own natural grassy and mountainous playgrounds.

Many people come to see Yellowstone to get away from cities with tall buildings and cars lined up on highways, for peace and quiet or just to see nature.

One reason that Yellowstone National Park is so special is because it was the first of all National Parks. Since then, the government has added many other parks, and historic and prehistoric sites called National Monuments, to the list of preserved places. There are now more than 400 spread all over the country that are taken care of by the National Park Service. The Park Service works hard to keep those places clean and friendly for people to visit.

Over time as Yellowstone became more beloved by Americans and other National Parks were set aside to be protected and nourished, people in other countries followed their lead. They looked at special places in their own nations and formed their own National Parks.

Also with the passing of many years people looked back at the creation of Yellowstone and the rest of the Parks and complimented the United States for doing this. It has often been said that starting a National Parks system was "America's best idea."

The United States is known throughout the world for freedoms for the people and many accomplishments in industry, business, sports, and art, so it is very flattering for others to say the National Parks are the best of all good things our country has done.

Chapter 1
Tribal Inhabitation

Long before it became the first National Park, Yellowstone had already attracted the attention of thousands of people. Native Americans were the first people to live in the area that came to be known as Yellowstone National Park. Different tribes had resided there for more than 10,000 years.

About 15,000 years ago during the Ice Age, all of what is now Yellowstone National Park was covered by glaciers. As the climate warmed, the glaciers retreated and left behind rivers and valleys that attracted mammoths and bison. Those mammoths and bison served as great food sources for early humans, who followed them to the Park.

Archeologists have been able to make a rough timeline of human life in the Park by studying tools that were left behind. Many of the hunting tools like knives, spears, and arrows were made out of obsidian. In the northwestern corner of the park stands the Obsidian Cliff, a ninety-eight foot-tall cliff of exposed obsidian rock. Since obsidian is made from magma or lava cooling into a black glass-like rock, it makes sense that there would be obsidian in the volcanic region of Yellowstone.

Archeologists can figure out exactly where a piece of obsidian came from by x-raying it. They were able to confirm that most of the obsidian tools found in Yellowstone and surrounding states were actually from the Obsidian Cliff.

While it's difficult for archeologists to pinpoint exactly which tribe left which tool, they can pinpoint roughly when it was left. Some of the tools found around Yellowstone Lake can be dated to over 9,000 years old, with many newer artifacts found as well. This matches up with some tribal oral histories.

Today, twenty-six tribes have been associated with Yellowstone National Park. This means that at least some of the lands, resources, or animals found inside the Park are historically connected to the tribe. The tribes inhabit reservations spread across eight states, though many were still in the area of Yellowstone when it was being explored.

Many of the artifacts found in Yellowstone are made from obsidian from the nearby cliffs.

The Shoshone tribe was the tribe seen the most often by European explorers. The explorers often wrote about finding small groups of Shoshone during their journeys. Other tribes would pass through the land to hunt or gather food. This included the Crow, Blackfeet, Salish, Kootenai, and Kiowa tribes.

After Yellowstone was declared a National Park, the United States Government relocated many of the tribes in an effort to make the Park feel safer for European-American visitors. The

Park Service spread a rumor that the Native Americans were scared of the Yellowstone area due to its volcanic activity and geothermal features. This wasn't true, however. Many of the tribes actually saw Yellowstone as sacred land and used the hot springs, mud pots, and geysers in ceremonies and rituals.

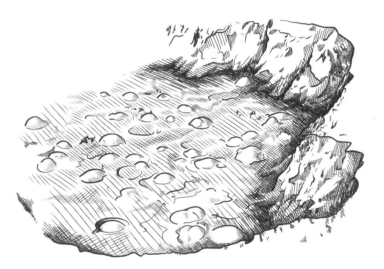

The most famous Yellowstone mud pots
are the Artist Paint Pots and the Fountain Paint Pots.

Chapter 2
European Exploration

In the early 1800s when the United States was a very young country, stories of the wild frontier began to be told by mountain men to people in the big cities.

In those days, there were no cars, railroads, airplanes, or telephones like we are all used to today. That meant it was very hard to take long trips across the countryside that had no roads. The only people who took those trips were men who hunted and trapped animals for food and furs. They saw the steam coming from the ground from what are now called geothermal features. When they told people they saw the land on fire, people thought they were liars. They were accused of making up stories, and people made fun of them. So they stopped talking about the things they saw.

The United States was such a rugged country that citizens did not really know what was out in the wilds west of the Mississippi River. In 1803, when Thomas Jefferson was president, he made a deal with France to buy 828,000 square miles of land for the United States. The sale was called "The Louisiana Purchase" and nearly doubled the size of the country.

President Jefferson did not know exactly what he bought, however, so he formed a team of explorers to travel to the West and find out. The Lewis and Clark Expedition was a very famous and important expedition in American history. It was named after two men, Meriwether Lewis and William Clark, who were the leaders. Between 1804 and 1806, this group of explorers mapped where they went, studied the geography, and learned what kind of birds and animals lived in the West.

One member of their party was named John Colter. When the expedition returned east, Colter did not go with the others. He stayed in the West and became known as a mountain man. He lived off the land by hunting, fishing, and trapping. As Colter moved around, he came upon the various hot springs of Yellowstone that were then unknown.

Colter is credited as being the first "mountain man" and the first European to see the Teton Mountain Range and what would become Yellowstone National Park.

He was credited with being the first person of European descent—non-Native American—to see the wonders of Yellowstone. He was also one of those people whose words were not believed.

Since no one else had ever seen such sights before, it was thought he made the whole thing up. Instead, because of his description of what he saw as "fire and brimstone," people viewed this as an imaginary place and began calling it "Colter's Hell."

Many years passed and more and more Americans came west. They traveled either by themselves or in small groups by horseback or wagon train to look for new places to settle down and start farming. Such movements slowed down drastically as the country experienced a horrible Civil War between 1860 and 1865. But once peace was established, the idea of moving

Henry Washburn led the Washburn Expedition exploring Yellowstone, which resulted in Mount Washburn being named after him.

west and expanding to new territory became popular again.

In 1869, three men on horseback from Montana explored a portion of what became the Park and kept diaries about what they saw. In 1870, the Washburn Expedition looked at a different area of the Park, guided by Army troops. The leader was Henry Washburn, who later had a 10,243-foot mountain named after him inside the Park.

The 1871 Hayden Expedition was the group that performed the greatest amount of exploring and brought back impressive photographs taken by William Henry Jackson and paintings by artist Thomas Moran. They were put on display in the US Capitol and regarded as proof of all the beautiful things in Yellowstone.

This established for all that the Yellowstone region was a place unique to the rest of the United States. Also, even as early as that, the first people were speaking up about the need to make sure some places remained wild. America had all of this space and that was one thing that made it different from countries in Europe and other places in the world. Those people were determined to preserve it.

John Muir is credited as the Father of the National Parks because of his letters, essays, and books that pushed for the preservation of the United States's wilderness.

The man who became most famous at this time for supporting the idea of conservation was named John Muir. He was born in 1838 and originally came from Scotland. He did not want to see America spoil all of its lands.

Muir first became well-known for getting the government interested in preserving what is now Yosemite National Park in California. He had a great big beard and strong opinions about what he thought was the right thing to do. He argued very hard to convince officials to protect the Yosemite Valley, and it was set aside for conservation by the government of California. This was before the establishment of Yellowstone.

Yosemite was the first place that the US government protected for public enjoyment, but they gave it to California to make into a state park, not a national park.

Through his writings and speeches, John Muir became known all over for his support of environmental causes. In 1892, Muir founded the Sierra Club, a famous organization that continues to support such causes today.

After the public and government authorities witnessed the photographs and paintings of the amazing sights of Yellowstone, Congress agreed to make it the first National Park. On March 1, 1872, President Ulysses S. Grant signed the legislation.

Soon after that, Nathaniel Langford, who had been so impressed by what he saw with Washburn on the 1871 exploration, was named the first superintendent of Yellowstone National Park. While this was a great distinction, Congress had not really done its job beyond actually creating the Park.

Langford fell in love with the area known as the Grand Canyon of the Yellowstone and the Upper and Lower Falls. The powerful waterfalls roared through a break in the mountains. Langford thought this was so beautiful that it almost did not seem real to him.

The first set of falls along the Yellowstone River,
the Upper Falls, stand 109 ft high.

The Senators and members of the House
of Representatives that made up Congress did
not pass another bill to provide any money to
either pay Langford or to run the Park. This
meant Yellowstone was officially preserved, but

there was no one there to enforce the rules. This lack of regulation made for a bad beginning for Yellowstone.

Chapter 3
<u>Growing Pains</u>

The creation of Yellowstone National Park was something important Congress did for the American people. But because Congress did not come up with a way to pay for running the Park, there were problems in the beginning.

Yellowstone was already becoming famous, but many bad men roamed the area. This was still a dangerous time on the American frontier. The West was not tamed. Anyone who traveled to that region might encounter robbers or run into Native American tribes who were not happy to see them. Much of Yellowstone was then called lawless. That meant there were no police or sheriffs to help if trouble broke out.

The government was also trying to move Native Americans in other parts of the county. Settlers wanted to farm and build homes on Native American ancestral land. To fill that desire, the US government created reservations for the Native American tribes and moved them off their ancestral lands to the reservations. Some tribes, like the Dakota tribe, made treaties and agreements with the government. Others, like the Nez Perce tribe, fought back. The American government built a system of forts to house men enlisted in the cavalry. Those riders wearing blue uniforms regularly fought against Indian tribes in what came to be called the Plains Indians Wars.

The Nez Perce tribe traveled from their homeland to Montana, where they made their final stand.

When the government tried to move the Nez Perce from their ancestral lands in Oregon, the tribe fled through Idaho, Wyoming, and Montana. Along the way, they fought the US Army at least six times. This was called the Nez Perce War, though now is better known as the Flight of the Nez Perce. During this time, the Nez Perce spent almost two weeks in what is now Yellowstone. The tribe encountered many park visitors, attacking some, and killing two.

Since the country was busy with the Plains Indians Wars, no one thought much of Yellowstone. No money was appropriated—Congress's name for paying for a project— and nobody was hired to run Yellowstone except Nathaniel Langford. He was given a big title to be the boss, but he was the boss of nobody. There were no workers to take care of things. Langford could not even afford to carry out his responsibilities. Because he wasn't being paid, he had to take a job somewhere else, so he barely even had time to visit Yellowstone.

Langford wrote a book about his experiences and he said he wanted to explore the Yellowstone, but it was too dangerous because of hostility with the Native tribes. He said that, much like John Colter in the distant past, what he saw was so impressive he worried people "on our return home" would not believe their descriptions of the wonders of Yellowstone either.

A painting of the Lower Falls of Yellowstone by Thomas Moran showed Americans how beautiful Yellowstone was.

The roaring Grand Canyon of the Yellowstone waterfalls were so gigantic, Langford said, "I realized my own littleness."

There was no tourism at the time either. Yellowstone was a very wild place and no roads led to the Park. So the government had established a Park for the people, but the people could not really get there.

Chapter 4
National Park Service

The government wanted to protect the wild animals living in the Park, too, but men who lived in the area did not respect the rules. Instead, they hunted at will, shooting as many of the bear, elk, and other animals as they wanted.

People were getting upset that this beautiful place was not being protected as the law read. In 1880, as an experiment, officials in Washington, D.C. came up with an idea. Although it seemed silly to think it would make much difference, the head of the Department of the Interior, which was in charge of protecting Yellowstone, hired one man to go to Yellowstone and patrol the 2.2 million acres on the people's behalf.

Much to the surprise of many people, this one man helped change things. His name was Harry Yount, and he was born in 1838. He had fought in the Civil War before becoming a hunter, gold prospector, and mountain man. He became a hero of sorts.

The National Park Service gives the Harry Yount Award
to the best park ranger each year in honor
of the country's first park ranger.

A very tough guy, Yount had learned how to
survive in wild lands and how to protect himself.
He had the nickname "Rocky Mountain Harry." It
was his job—and he was paid $1,000—to prevent

people from breaking the rules. Harry Yount's job was called gamekeeper. In later years, after the National Park Service was created, people began calling Yount the first Park Ranger.

The biggest problem in Yellowstone at the time was poaching. Hunters went where they were not supposed to be and shot many more animals than they needed to eat. They were ruining the whole idea of preserving the Park for future generations.

Yount went off to live by himself in the Park in very primitive conditions. If he wanted to sleep anywhere but outdoors or in a tent, he had to build his own log cabin. He traveled around the Park looking for lawbreakers, which was a very risky job. There was always a threat someone might shoot Yount.

"He was the first man to weather a winter in Yellowstone," said Horace M. Albright, one of the Park's most influential superintendents. Winter in Yellowstone can be very harsh. It snows a lot and the winds blow so hard they can knock a person down. It gets colder than most places in the rest of the United States, sometimes even colder than Alaska. At one point, Yount's thermometer broke, so he could not even keep track of how cold it was.

Yellowstone is just as beautiful in winter, but many of the areas are inaccessible without a snowmobile.

For fourteen months in 1880 and 1881, Yount lived and traveled on his own. During that time, he kept records and made reports to the government, making suggestions on how to protect the land from vandals and the animals from rule-breakers. It was very obvious that one man could not be everywhere at once in the Park.

It was much too big. Yount recommended to his bosses that they create a police force.

Instead, as the wars on the Plains came to a conclusion, the US cavalry was assigned to supervise the activity in Yellowstone. Between 1886 and 1916, the cavalry kept the peace and made sure those poachers and other rule-breakers were controlled.

The army built what came to be called Fort Yellowstone at Mammoth Hot Springs. They also built sixty other buildings, some of wood and some of sandstone. Mammoth Hot Springs is at the far northern edge of Yellowstone, and the headquarters of the National Park Service supervising the Park remains there today. Many of the structures left behind by the army are still used. The rugged sandstone buildings house many offices.

It took about thirty-five years before the federal government listened to Yount's advice. In 1916, Congress created the National Park Service to supervise not only Yellowstone, but other National Parks that were coming into existence. The National Park Service protected eight parks in six states, most in neighboring states to Yellowstone National Park.

The rangers took their style of dress from the cavalry uniforms of the men who had protected the park before. Yount was the first ranger, but the men and women who came after him paved the way for the friendly journeys taken to the Park by millions of American families today.

Chapter 5
<u>Tourism</u>

Theodore Roosevelt once said, "There can be nothing in the world more beautiful than the . . . Canyon of the Yellowstone."

The whole idea behind making Yellowstone into a National Park was so it would always be there for people who wanted to see it. Congress's stated intent was to make sure Yellowstone would exist "For the Benefit and Enjoyment of the People." That sentence is written in stone on the Roosevelt Arch (named for former president Theodore Roosevelt) at the North Entrance to Yellowstone.

The problem was that in 1872, and for many years afterward, there were no roads or train tracks to that part of the United States. It was very hard to get there to experience the benefits.

For many people it seemed just about as hard to go to Yellowstone National Park as it would be to take a trip to the moon. It took until the beginning of the twentieth century, about thirty years after Yellowstone was created, before people began visiting the Park casually.

Early tourists would come to see the wonders of Yellowstone, but were disappointed by the Army management and their lack of knowledge.

For many people living in big cities, Yellowstone was a mystery. They knew it was supposed to be a wonderful place, but few people they knew had been there. In 1902, a song was written about the Park called "We'll Meet You Out in Yellowstone Park." The song helped encourage Americans to go check things out.

Yellowstone National Park started to keep track of how many people came to see the Park in 1904. That year a little more than 13,000 people showed up to see the animals and nature. It was not a larger number, but it was a start.

In the very early days, visitors had to rough it. They often camped in tents and even had to hunt for their own food. There were other dangers in the 1870s and 1880s. A group of nine people from Montana took a trip to the Park and were surprised by one adventure. "All in all, George Cowan's vacation to Yellowstone National Park had been going very well," one author wrote, "until the Indians shot him." Cowan had refused to give food to some Nez Perce tribesmen who were being chased by the cavalry, and they were not happy with him.

The Lake Hotel has recently received the Green Seal Gold certification, meaning it is very environmentaly friendly.

However, in 1891, the Lake Hotel, located overlooking Yellowstone Lake, was built to give travelers a place to stay. The three-story building was the type of large hotel more regularly seen in larger cities, not the wilderness.

A very important part of getting people to visit Yellowstone was the construction of railroad tracks right up to the front gate. By 1902, the Northern Pacific Railroad had train service to

Gardiner, Montana, right at the North Entrance. The tourists brought by the trains climbed into buggies—horse-drawn carriages—that carried them along dirt roads through the Park at a slow pace. Some rode in stagecoaches with drivers and guides to tell them what they were seeing. Tall mountains rose to the sky next to them. Wild animals trotted across their paths.

The Old Faithful Inn is considered the largest building in the world built from logs.

In 1904, a very famous American building opened in Yellowstone National Park. The Old Faithful Inn was a hotel, too, and was considered modern for the day because it had electricity and steam heat. Although it was a log building, made from the lodgepole pines that grow all over the Park, it had a huge stone fireplace.

By 1908, the Union Pacific Railroad was able to bring passengers right up to the Park's West Entrance in West Yellowstone, Montana. In 1912, the Chicago, Burlington & Pacific Railroad began bringing people to the East Entrance of the Park.

Once the National Park had such nice hotels to spend the night in, it was hoped more people would come to Yellowstone. The trains made that possible. Advertisements told people they could ride in comfort, look at the scenery, go fishing, take hikes, and see other special nature sights they could not see at home.

When Stephen Mather became the first director of the Park Service, he worked extra hard to get Americans to visit Yellowstone National Park. He wanted people to have fun and take advantage of what had been provided for them.

"We are merely servants of the people and are out to serve them," Mather said. "We are not owners of the areas, but merely custodians."

This was Mather's way of reminding Americans, government workers, and Park

Service employees that the American people owned the National Parks, and the rangers were taking care of them for the people.

The story is that, after Mather complained about how the national parks were being run, a frustrated Secretary of the Interior told him "If you don't like the way the parks are being run, come on down to Washington and run them yourself."

Over time more and more people visited Yellowstone and the other Parks. In 1915, as the nation changed from horseback riding to cars, the first automobiles were officially allowed into the Park. This began a tradition that continues today. Parents loaded up the whole family into the car and drove their own vehicles across the country from their homes right into the Park. Stagecoaches were no longer needed.

After the age of wagons and buggies passed and automobiles took over the Park, private transportation was available to visitors if they wanted to rent space in yellow touring cars. These fancy vehicles are extra-long, comfortable cars for six or more people used for taking in-Park trips while the passengers look out the windows.

Only about 500 snowmobiles are allowed in the park each day to lower the amount of noise and exhaust they make.

Visitors are in for a different experience if they visit in the winter. Yellowstone can be one of the coldest places in the United States. It snows so much in the Park that most of the roads are covered in white and not open to cars and trucks for months over the winter. Most of the millions of people who visit Yellowstone come in the spring and summer, though many thousands still do take trips to the Park in wintertime.

The Park is beautiful when all of the trees and mountains are covered with snow and ice. Visitors cannot go fishing, but they can take rides on snowmobiles or take cross-country ski trips to explore. Even more interesting for many people is the chance to take a ride inside the Park in a snow coach. These are heated vehicles, like buses, but they have tread like tanks instead of wheels like cars, so they won't get stuck in the snow.

From December to March, the only way to see Yellowstone is by snowcoach, snowmobile, or skis.

The park system has expanded to include fifty-nine National Parks, and by 2016, more than 300 million people per year visited a Park. In 2016, more than four million people took visits to Yellowstone National Park. As always, the visitors came to see what was out there, and to see the same things their parents and grandparents saw in Yellowstone many years earlier.

Yellowstone does not forget kids now, either. Children, usually between the ages of five and thirteen, can gain the tag of junior ranger by working to obtain badges as they travel through the Park. There are also booklets written especially for kids to read. A junior ranger recites an oath: "Explore, Learn and Protect!" They are promising to learn more about the National Parks, visit more of them, and help protect them from people who might throw trash on the ground or break signs or other Park things.

Going to Yellowstone National Park became the Great American Vacation, the one available to all Americans. By traveling to Yellowstone, people from all over the country, no matter where they lived, could share that experience.

Junior Rangers learn about things like park resources,
geothermal geology, wildlife, and fire ecology.

Chapter 6
Old Faithful and Geysers

There are more than 10,000 geothermal features in Yellowstone, more than anywhere else in the world. They are formed where rainwater and melting snow seep deep into the ground. Then, because much of the land underground inside Yellowstone is super-heated by a volcano, the water gets very hot, boils, and erupts back up through the surface.

Sometimes, these places send up steam that almost looks like smoke from a fire. Other times, they shoot water high into the air far above people's heads.

This water can be more than 200 degrees Fahrenheit and is very dangerous to go near. People can be scalded to death if they get too close, so the Park Service built wooden walkways inside Yellowstone for visitors to walk along for their safety. They can admire these hot areas that are so interesting to watch. Even if the water looks pretty, these are all areas where people should definitely not think about going swimming.

The most famous geyser in the park is called Old Faithful. It was given this name in 1870 by Henry Washburn, who led one of the early explorations into the Park. One day his group was traveling and came across water shooting into the air more than 100 feet. The group spent some time next to it and realized that the water burst from the ground at about the same time every hour. Because the timing was so reliable, Washburn named the geyser "Old Faithful."

Old Faithful was the first geyser in Yellowstone to be named by European explorers.

Later, Nathaniel P. Langford, the Park's first superintendent, wrote about being amazed when he first saw Old Faithful. He called it "an immense volume of clear, sparkling water projected into the air."

Since then, the land has changed and the ground has shifted. This put Old Faithful on a slightly different schedule. It still erupts very reliably, but closer to every seventy-five minutes rather than every sixty minutes. Every time Old Faithful erupts, it is a big occasion. During the summer months when the Park is crowded, sometimes 1,000 people watch Old Faithful go off.

More than any other geological feature in Yellowstone, about 145 years after the Park was founded, people still rate Old Faithful as the most important thing new visitors must see when they visit.

That was true from the beginning, and in 1877, a group of people camped near Old Faithful. While they were there they decided to experiment and see if the boiling water of an eruption would clean their laundry. So they stuffed all of their clothes into a pillow case. When Old Faithful began making noise, they threw the bag of clothes in the top. A few minutes passed before, all of a sudden, the water blew 100 feet in the air and heaved their clothes all over the place. They were lucky to find all the pieces.

As the tallest geyser in the world, Steamboat Geyser can erupt more than 300 feet in the air.

Nine geyser basins are spread around the Park, and each one of those areas has many geysers. About 1,300 geysers can be found inside Yellowstone. Old Faithful is the most famous geyser, but there are other special ones in the Park, too. Steamboat Glacier is located in the Norris Geyser Basin, and when it erupts, it propels water 300 feet in the air, higher than any other geyser in the world. No one really knows when Steamboat will erupt, though, so people don't gather around it. Between 1911 and 1961, it did not erupt even one time.

There are geothermal features all over Yellowstone National Park. A family can be driving along the Park road in a car and see steam coming up out of the ground in many places from hot springs. The most famous hot spring is the Grand Prismatic Spring. It is the largest in the United States and third largest in the world at 370 feet wide and 121 feet deep.

The Grand Prismatic Spring is more colorful than other hot springs. The water is a deep blue color in the middle, with reds, oranges, and

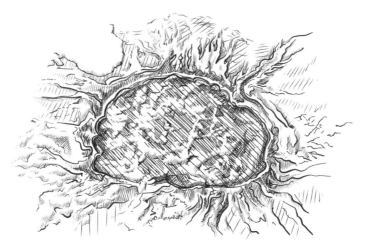

The Grand Prismatic Spring is the largest hot spring in the United States, and the third largest in the world.

yellows on the outside. These colors are caused by different bacteria that live in the water. At the center, the water is the hottest, and the bacteria cannot survive. As the water cools, though, different bacteria can grow and thrive, each with its own color.

Mammoth Hot Springs, one of the busiest areas of the Park, is the location of the Travertine Terraces. Travertine is a type of limestone, a strong calcium-based rock. The water from the spring has a mineral called calcium carbonate in it. When the carbonate mixes with oxygen, it makes the terraces look white. While the

Travertine Terraces may look fun to climb on, the water's temperature is more than 160 degrees Fahrenheit and can severely burn skin.

The steps of Mammoth Hot Springs are made of travertine, a type of limestone that is usually created near hot springs.

Other geothermal features include fumaroles and mud pots. Fumaroles make noise. The steam is hotter at a fumarole, which has less water in it, and when it lets off steam, it hisses. Mud pots smell bad to people. They produce Sulphur, which smells like rotting eggs. Usually people can smell them from a great distance away. Because there is a lot of acid in the water, they also bubble.

These are many different kinds of hot spots that families can see as they drive around Yellowstone National Park. What people cannot see is the Yellowstone supervolcano because it is deep below the surface of the Earth.

Fumaroles are the hottest geothermal feature in Yellowstone, sometimes reaching as high as 280 degrees Fahrenheit.

Just above the volcano is an area that was formed by volcanic eruptions called a caldera. A caldera forms when a volcano erupts so much that it runs out of lava. Without the lava, the volcano collapses in on itself, creating a large crater.

Three huge eruptions created Yellowstone Caldera, but the last one was 630,000 years ago, long before any people lived in the area. Some other eruptions helped form lakes. The last eruption large enough to produce flowing lava happened 70,000 years ago.

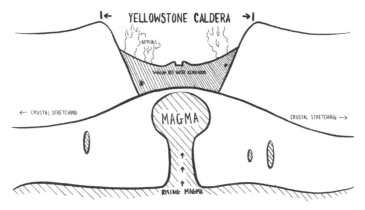

YELLOWSTONE CALDERA

GEYSERS

SHALLOW HOT WATER RESERVOIRS

← CRUSTAL STRETCHING

MAGMA

CRUSTAL STRETCHING →

RISING MAGMA

Rising magma heats the water in the caldera, causing hot springs, geysers, fumaroles, and mudpots.

Some people worry that Yellowstone could explode someday, but scientists say this is unlikely to occur for thousands of years. Right now, it remains safe to go see Old Faithful and other geysers.

Chapter 7
Bison

One of the biggest treats for visitors of Yellowstone National Park is seeing large numbers of bison roaming through the Park. These huge animals are more popularly called buffalo, but their scientific name is bison. Regardless of which name people like best, it is bit of a miracle that between 3,500 and 4,500 buffalo live in the Park at any one time.

"There is no other place you can see them in this abundance," said Rick Wallen, a biologist with the National Park Service inside Yellowstone.

People who drive through the Lamar Valley near the Northeast Gate of Yellowstone can usually see hundreds of bison, sometimes it even seems like 1,000. It reminds visitors of earlier times in American history when there were millions of bison spread out across the American West.

At certain times of year, especially in spring, it can be an even bigger thrill to see the huge bison mommas with their new babies. Since bison grow to be so big, when they are born, they already weigh about fifty pounds. These bison calves have more of a reddish color than the brown fur they will grow into.

Bison babies weigh about fifty pounds at birth and are commonly called "red dogs."

Many people consider bison to be very beautiful and impressive animals. Fully grown males can weigh 2000 pounds, fifteen times as much as the average middle schooler. They have huge heads with horns; powerful bodies and legs; shaggy, beard-like hair under their chins; and thick coats that keep them warm in the winter. They can run very fast if they want to, but usually they just walk around taking advantage of grasses to eat. They do not charge at visitors unless people make the mistake of getting too close to the bison and bothering them or threatening their babies. That is a big no-no.

A male bison can weigh more than a ton (2,000 pounds), so making one angry isn't a smart idea!

If people do that, they can be in trouble. When a bison gets mad, it might run at a person. They can easily knock people over or gore them with a horn. That could send people to the hospital. Yellowstone National Park warns visitors not to get too close and to leave bison alone to enjoy their lives.

There was a time in the 1800s when bison herds could be seen all over the Great Plains areas of North Dakota, South Dakota, Wyoming, Montana, Kansas, Colorado, and a few other states. At one time, buffalo were seen in the wild everywhere between Mexico and Canada. There were so many of them that nobody could count them all, but experts guess there might have been between thirty and sixty million. It seemed as if there were so many bison that there was enough to feed the whole United States forever.

Most bison herds are made up of females and their babies, while males live in smaller groups nearby.

The buffalo were particularly important to local Native American tribes. To some of those tribes, like the Lakota, buffalo were sacred symbols of their religion. Many tribes still hunted the animals to provide meat for their families. They also used their thick hides to make heavy coats to stay warm in the winter. The bison survived by eating the large supply of grasses available on the Plains, and they could eat a lot every day.

However, the American government then made a very bad decision. The officials declared it legal for hunters and soldiers to kill as many bison as they wanted, many more than they needed for food.

By eliminating the bison, Native Americans that depended on bison would be forced to change their way of life and move away from their old homes. This also encouraged European American people to move to the West and settle as farmers and ranchers. They replaced the grass fields that fed the buffalo with fields for crops and livestock.

During a few short decades of the nineteenth century, almost all of the bison in the country were killed. By 1900, the American buffalo was very close to being eliminated from the planet and going extinct. Now, people consider what happened to the buffalo a crime. They say it never should have happened. At the time, though, the importance of preserving species wasn't well understood and the buffalo was almost allowed to die out.

In total, over 24 million bison would be killed, leaving less than 1,000 bison in North America.

Although many people wanted to do so, this situation was almost impossible to fix. It was believed when the twentieth century began that there might only be about 400 bison left. All of the rest of the millions had been killed.

When all of the killing stopped, there were twenty-five buffalo still alive in Yellowstone National Park. That small number was allowed to continue living inside the Park, and from that little herd the population grew again. Those twenty-five buffalo are the base of the family tree, the direct ancestors of the bison which survived and still live in the Park.

In 1905, because certain people believed the government made a mistake allowing the bison to be killed, the American Bison Society was founded. More than a century later, 500,000 bison live under the care of humans on private land, and another 30,000 live on publicly-owned land like Yellowstone. Of those, 19,000 are the old-style bison from the Plains. Another 11,000 are wood bison, a kind of buffalo that is slightly different. Wood bison are bigger with larger horns. At least some bison now live in all fifty states.

Founded by Theodore Roosevelt in 1905, the American Bison Society worked to prevent the extinction of the American bison.

In May of 2016, President Barack Obama signed a new law. The National Bison Legacy Act turned the bison into the United States' National Mammal. The bison then held a special status of appreciation by the same government that once tried to kill all of them.

Bison have a special place in the hearts of many people of the West. They cannot be petted like dogs or cats, but their presence in places like Yellowstone National Park means they can still be looked at and admired. That would have been doubtful 100 years ago.

Chapter 8
Bears

In the early days of the twentieth century, Yellowstone National Park was still trying to bring more tourists to the wilds. One thing visitors were promised and expected to see was a bear show.

Every night, a cart carrying garbage was pulled by horses to a predetermined area. Rangers set out hotel trash to feed dinner to grizzly bears. Visitors gathered nearby to watch and take photographs. This was a very different time, and that type of interaction between people and bears later became against the rules. At that time, though, nobody minded or understood this program could be dangerous. People didn't think about the fact that feeding the bears could be bad for them. They might not be able to take care of themselves in the wild without the help of humans.

The "Lunch Counter" hosted meals for bears serving Yellowstone hotel garbage. This put both visitors and the bears in danger.

For many years inside Yellowstone, rangers and other workers actually supervised the bear feeding. There was a fenced-in area called "the lunch counter" where garbage was distributed for bears in the middle of the day, too. People watched the animals get fed at these times as if it was all happening at the circus.

The visitors seemed to look at the bears more as pets than wild animals. Sometimes when people stopped to picnic, bears would come up to them at their tables and beg for more food. These people would feed the bears by hand. This could be very dangerous because the bears were not careful and could bite someone's finger or a hand. People would run out of food while a bear was still hungry, and the bear might want more. Then the bear they had just fed might turn on them and angrily attack the people.

In later years, bears walked up to the open windows of cars, raised themselves on hind legs, leaned their paws on the car, and begged for food. Bears were not fussy and would eat anything.

Bears would intentially stop cars to beg
Yellowstone visitors for food.

Conservation managers learned quite some time ago this was all a bad idea. What bears were really supposed to eat, what was healthiest for them, was the bark from pine trees, grasses, nuts, and animals. It was bad for them to eat candy bars or cereal.

In the early days of the National Park Service, the agency had to keep working to convince Congress to give it money to stay in business. The more people who came to visit the Parks, the more popular the Congressmen would think Yellowstone was. The more popular it was, the more Congress would be willing to pay the bills.

Yellowstone was really the only place in the country visitors could come to see bears up close. The Park Service officials wanted them to see bears and go home and tell their neighbors how great it was. That way the neighbors would come to Yellowstone the next year.

Horace M. Albright, the second director of the Park Service, who also worked as superintendent of Yellowstone National Park, wanted people to get as up-close to the animals as they could. He believed feeding the bears in front of the visitors was the best thing to do. Although it sounds crazy, Albright even said if a visitor got a scar from a bear bite or claw while feeding one of the animals, it would make a great souvenir.

Horace Albright held many jobs within the
National Park Service, including legal assistant,
acting director, and superintendent.

The bears were smarter than the people,
though. Once more and more cars started
driving into Yellowstone, the bears were no longer
satisfied just getting their organized meals from
the Park hotels' garbage. They wanted to eat
more often. Bears actually began blocking the
roads in front of cars and demanding food from
the drivers and passengers. Instead of staying in
the forest where their homes should have been,
the bears came out on the highways to beg.

More injuries occurred when bears bit people, scratched them, or just trampled them. It was surprising more people were not killed. By 1931, Park officials recorded forty-eight people each year being harmed by bears. They recorded another 100 cases where bears destroyed property.

It wasn't until 1960 that the Park Service began to change the rules. By 1970, very strict rules were in place to separate people and bears. Instead of bears being given garbage, the hotels in the Park had to put their garbage in containers which bears could not break into. Garbage dumps were closed. Visitors were forbidden to feed bears.

The officials also had to break bears of their bad habits. The bears kept coming around people looking for food, so rangers relocated bears away from buildings and roads for their own good. Sometimes, when bears kept coming back, the Park Service had to put them down. While sad, it was the safest for both the visitors and the bears.

Yellowstone began educating people about the dangers of feeding the bears and posted many signs warning against it.

The people who worked in Yellowstone did not want the bears to disappear. They wanted them to be happy in the wilderness. Bears had lived in Yellowstone National Park and the area around it for centuries. Yet the number of bears in the Yellowstone area dropped to just 136 by 1973. Then the federal government stepped in.

The United States has a law called the Endangered Species Act that helps prevent fish, animals, or plants from all going extinct. The grizzly bears in the area were having the same kind of tough problem surviving that the buffalo did.

It took a long time, but, because of the work done to save the grizzly bears in the area, by the summer of 2017, the number had bounced back up to about 700. Just like the bison, they have made a healthy comeback.

Bear cubs stay with their mothers until they are about two years old, then they leave to find their own territory.

Chapter 9
Gray Wolves

It helps to bring a very powerful telescope or camera to Yellowstone National Park if you hope to see a wolf in the wild. Either that or you must be very lucky and happen to be driving in a car or hiking in the woods at a time when one of the Park's gray wolves shows up.

There are different kinds of wolves, but the wolf that lives in Yellowstone is called the gray wolf. The gray wolf usually has gray fur, as might be expected, but there are also white and black wolves that are part of the species. There are many fewer of those colors than gray, however.

There are usually five to eight wolves in a pack, but can be up to thirty or more depending on food and habitat.

Many people say wolves look just like big dogs. Wolves are not pets, though, and are not as friendly as dogs. They are bigger than most kinds of dogs, sometimes weighing 140 pounds. Wolves are not domesticated, meaning they are not tamed, and will really hurt someone if they feel threatened. They belong in the wild.

Of the large animals—grizzly bears, black bears, bison, elk, and mule deer—that can be seen inside the Park, it is the wolf that is the hardest to see, even if you carry binoculars. The wolves of Yellowstone try to stay out of sight. It is as if they are always "it" in a game of hide and seek and try not to be found.

From the standpoint of history, however, Americans are very lucky there are any wolves to ever see in Yellowstone. At one time, the Park Service wanted to get rid of all of the wolves and tried very hard to do so. They would have been happy if there were no wolves left anywhere on planet Earth.

Even at the time the Park was created, wolves were having a tough time in the territories of

Wyoming, Montana, and Idaho. There had once been hundreds of thousands of gray wolves living in America. However as the country grew, people wanted to expand west. If wolves got in their way, they were killed off. Just as importantly, as people built ranches and farms and settled down in more rural places, they built on top of the old grasslands where wolves liked to roam. This meant that wolves were wandering through people's farms, and they were not welcome.

Many wolves were shot by ranchers defending their livestock.

The people moving west needed to eat too, so while they were setting up their farms, they killed local animals for food. Unfortunately, many of the animals they killed, the wolves also ate. So there was a lot less food for the wolves.

It was just like what happened to the bison on the Great Plains. Wolves were pushed out of their favorite places, and the population got smaller and smaller. Nobody came to the defense of the wolves, and slowly they began to die off.

The gray wolf should have been safe inside Yellowstone National Park, but the government decided the Park, and other animals inside the Park, would be better off without them.

While Yellowstone was created and being preserved for the future for good reasons, the idea that wolves were bad took hold. It was against the law to hunt bears, bison, elk, moose, and other big animals in the Park, but it was legal to hunt wolves. Some scientists at the time thought wolves were the enemy of elk, deer, and other animals in the Park because they ate them. It was thought that the Park would be better off if wolves were removed.

The ranchers in the West who had taken over much of the wolves' old areas hated them. The ranchers raised cattle and sheep. Since there wasn't enough of the wolves' natural food to feed them all, they started eating the livestock. The ranchers thought too many of their privately owned animals were being killed and eaten by wolves and coyotes. In 1907, they convinced the US Fish and Wildlife Service that they were right. In that year alone under the new hunting laws, 1,800 wolves and 23,000 coyotes were killed in National Forests. Hunters were paid between twenty and fifty dollars for each dead wolf.

Killing wolves meant that the elk had no natural predator, allowing them to overpopulate.

From then on, it was basically open season on wolves just about everywhere. That included inside Yellowstone National Park, where it was thought wolves and animals would be safe. By 1926, the National Park Service believed it had killed every gray wolf that lived in the Park. The damage was done.

For many years after that, people reported seeing wolves here and there in the Park, but they were only seen one or two at a time, and no one could be sure these visitors were really seeing wolves. However, there were so many wolf sightings reported that some of them had to be real. The government believed any wolf seen inside Yellowstone was just passing through from one state to another and didn't live in the park.

Over time, conservationists convinced the government it was wrong to kill the wolves. Studies showed it would be better for the Park and the other animals if there were wolves living there after all. Removing the wolves started a chain reaction that hurt a lot of the animals in the Park. Now the beavers were in danger too. The conservationists argued that the wolves had been unfairly removed from Yellowstone. The only way to fix the problem was to bring gray wolves back.

So the Park Service started over. In a very unusual program, the government decided to bring wolves back to Yellowstone. This is called "re-introduction." In January of 1995, Canadian officials trapped fourteen gray wolves to be shipped to Yellowstone National Park. They were released into the wild in March. The next year, 1996, another seventeen wolves were brought from Canada to Yellowstone.

The reintroduction of wolves has saved
Yellowstone's beavers and willow trees.

Over the last twenty years or so, wolves increased in numbers and have regained their normal place in Yellowstone. It is now thought there are about 100 wolves living in the Park. They are protected under the law, and it is illegal to hunt them. The program is considered to be a great success and the amount of wolves living outside Yellowstone in Wyoming, Montana, and Idaho has also increased.

It took a long time, but the people who run Yellowstone National Park accomplished something very rare. It was almost as if they were able to go back in history with a time machine to undo something people living nearly 100 years ago thought was a permanent change. Instead, as long as they have a telescope, Americans now have the chance to enjoy the sight of wolves in their Park, something Americans living in 1927 could not say.

Chapter 10
Forest Fires

Fire roaring through a forest can be scary. The hot orange flames burn up trees and brush on the ground and chase animals from their hiding places. Flames can be incredibly hot and burn buildings, sending large clouds of smoke into the sky.

Once a fire starts, it can be hard to stop, especially in a place filled with forests like Yellowstone National Park. The trees are close together, which makes it easier for flames to keep moving, especially if it is very windy. Wind can be a firefighter's worst enemy.

One thing that can be dangerous about living in the western states is the summer fire season. If the weather gets very hot for a while and the air is dry, as it is in many parts of the West, the smallest spark can start a fire in the woods.

Campfires that are left unattended or not properly extinguished can start wildfires very quickly.

If a person throws a match away after lighting a cigarette and the match lands on dry grass, it can start a fire and that fire can spread very quickly. When visitors come to Yellowstone, they are warned to be careful if they start camp fires to cook their food or keep warm at night. There are rules telling them not to light fires in certain areas.

However, even a legal camp fire can result in a major forest fire if a visitor does not stomp it out completely when he is done. Although the fire may look as if it is out, if even a small amount of embers stay hot in a camp fire, it can flame up again and spread after the people leave it behind.

Natural fires in Yellowstone are started by lightning strikes.

Even more often, the cause of forest fires inside Yellowstone National Park is lightning hitting a tree or dry brush in a wilderness area where there are no campgrounds or trails where people go regularly. Sometimes that means a Park Ranger will not see a fire burning until it has grown large.

Forest fires happen every year in Yellowstone. Sometimes they are so bad that roads must be closed to visitors and they have to drive all the way around to different roads to get where they want to go. Sometimes even one of the Park entrances will be closed for a little while because it is important for National Park Service's firefighters to take over the roads and put the fires out.

Fires have always occurred in the West. Before the land was settled, they did not come near people and just burned out when it rained or snowed. Because Yellowstone is a public Park, the Park Service keeps track of every fire to help keep everyone safe.

One thing Park Rangers can't do is control the weather. They get worried if fires start and keep growing to the point they cannot be put out. It won't matter how many firefighters try to do so or how much water is dumped on the blazes. Sometimes helicopters are used to scoop up water from Yellowstone Lake and fly back to the fires and dump the water from the sky. This plan is used if fires are in the backwoods and the firefighters cannot drive their fire engines close enough to shoot the water from their hoses.

Some years, there are hardly any forest fires inside Yellowstone National Park, but in 1988, the fire season was the worst since the area became a Park in 1872. Yellowstone is 2.2 million

From June to September of 1988, 59 fires burned almost 800,000 acres of Yellowstone.

acres, and more than 793,880 acres caught fire that summer. That is one-third of the entire Park. Nothing like that had ever happened before, and nothing like it has ever happened since.

Many people were angry the Park they loved suffered so much damage. Almost everywhere they looked, trees were burned black, lost their leaves, tumbled to the ground, or were stripped of their bark. They looked the same way logs put on a fireplace look after the fire is out.

The Park Service has fire spotters all around the Park, and through the use of computers and other systems they monitor the entire Park all of the time to try and spot a fire right after it starts. That is not always possible to do, and the officials' equipment wasn't as good thirty years ago as it is today.

That year, the smoke from a fire—the beginning of these huge blazes—was first seen near the South Entrance to Yellowstone, not far from Shoshone Lake. That gate connects Yellowstone to Grand Teton National Park and

Yellowstone's rangers keep a close watch for signs of fires to prevent excessive damage.

the community of Jackson Hole, Wyoming. The fire report came in on the afternoon of June 23, 1988. Nobody could imagine the size of the problem just beginning.

What began small kept growing. It had been a dry summer, and fighting the fire was complicated by high winds. The giant fire could not be contained which led to the entire Park being closed to the public for the first time in its history on September 8. As many as

9,000 firefighters at one time, with the help of helicopters and airplanes, were on the job trying to kill the fires.

Forest fires clear a lot of the shrubs and grasses, but many trees can survive smaller fires.

There had never been anything like it before in Yellowstone. Four thousand military men and women were brought in to help the firefighters. It cost $120 million just to put out the fires, and the people involved in stopping them were amazed by what they saw.

"I'll always remember Yellowstone," a California firefighter named Curt Folsom said, "knowing there was nothing we could do to stop these fires."

Many people viewed the entire experience as a horrible disaster. However, wildfires serve a purpose in nature. They help renew the land and plants. Part of the firefighting plan for the future was to let fires in the back country burn for regrowth as long as they did not threaten people or buildings. Sometimes hard decisions must be made.

When a forest is burned, the new plants that grow aren't always the same ones that were burned.

In 2016, fires seemed to break out all over Yellowstone once more, and people feared it was going to be 1988 all over again. That did not happen, but 63,000 acres did burn, the most since the 793,880 of nearly thirty years earlier. While they had to cope with smoke in many areas of the Park, at no time that year were tourists turned away from visiting Yellowstone because of fires.

Chapter 11
Fishing and Boating

One of the oldest traditions in Yellowstone National Park is fishing. People fished in the area before it was a Park, and kept on fishing after it became a Park in 1872.

Although there are several kinds of fish living in the lakes and rivers of Yellowstone, the best-known and most popular is the cutthroat trout. Cutthroat trout have always been in the Park. They were there long before people came to fish, and they are still there today.

Fishermen find certain kinds of fish in different parts of the United States. Bass and perch are all over the country. Tarpon are very big fish that are most commonly caught in Florida. People travel to Alaska to catch big king salmon. They come to Yellowstone to fish for cutthroat trout.

You will not find cutthroat trout off the shore of Massachusetts or in the Gulf Coast near Louisiana. They are members of the salmon family, but they come from the Pacific Ocean. They are found in mountain streams of the Rocky Mountains and western states like Wyoming, Utah, and Oregon. This area includes Yellowstone National Park. These are their home areas because they are happiest living in cold water.

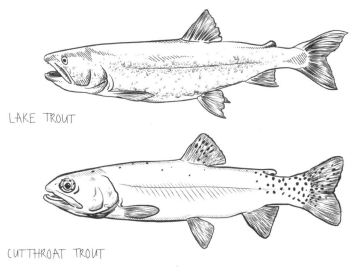

LAKE TROUT

CUTTHROAT TROUT

More than 2.4 million lake trout have been removed
from Yellowstone Lake since 1994
in an effort to protect the Cutthroat Trout.

Including cutthroat trout, there are nineteen types of fish that live in Park waters. Other fish include rainbow trout, brook trout, brown trout, whitefish, and arctic grayling. Thirteen of the fish have always been in the Park. The other six were brought to the Park by people over the years.

The reason behind the cutthroat trout's name is a colorful red slash across its jaws. In the early decades of Yellowstone, one of fishermen's favorite things to do was catch cutthroat trout and eat the fish for dinner while camping. However, over time too many fishermen came to Yellowstone and caught too many cutthroat trout. Just like buffalo and wolves, people were afraid that all of the cutthroat trout would be captured and eaten. If that happened, it would be the end of fishing in Yellowstone.

To help protect cutthroat trout, who lay eggs below the bridge, fishing from Fishing Bridge was banned in 1973.

For decades in the 1900s, one popular place for fishing was a place called Fishing Bridge. Fishermen used to stand on the bridge and cast into the water below. Over time, they caught so many fish there that it was possible the trout would run out. So the Park Service decided there would be no more fishing from that spot. People can still walk along sidewalks at the bridge, as long as they aren't fishing, and look down and see trout swimming below.

There are many bodies of water in Yellowstone. Some of the biggest and most famous ones are the Yellowstone River, which the Park area is named for; the Madison River; the Gibbon River; the Lamar River; the Gallatin River; and the Firehole River. The largest body of water in Yellowstone is Yellowstone Lake, which has its own special history.

Yellowstone Lake is filled with fresh water, not salt water like the oceans. It is the biggest lake in North America located at higher than 7,000 feet of elevation. Yellowstone Lake is at 7,732 feet.

That is more than a mile high, higher up than the city of Denver, Colorado. There are many mountains in the United States that are less than 7,000 feet tall.

Yellowstone Lake has been called Yellow Stone, Eustis Lake, and Sublette's Lake throughout history.

Yellowstone Lake is 136 square miles in size, which means that, just standing next to it, you cannot see to the other side in most places. The deepest spot in Yellowstone Lake is 390 feet deep. That's deep enough that you can't see the bottom. There are 110 miles of shoreline, which is about the distance from Hartford, Connecticut to New York City, so people cannot walk around it all at once. A lot of the shoreline is very rugged, too, blocked by trees and rocks.

What people can do in summer—and have done for more than a century—is fish on the lake and take boat rides after the ice melts. It gets so cold in Yellowstone National Park in winter that the lake freezes and turns to ice three feet thick. Since the land around Yellowstone Lake is so beautiful and the water is so pretty, visitors to Yellowstone enjoy getting out on the water once

Hayden Survey sailed the first boat on Yellowstone Lake, called Annie.

it warms up.

Records show the first time anyone ever took a boat ride for pleasure on Yellowstone Lake was in 1874, when two men climbed into a rowboat and pushed off into the water. In 1889, a man whose name was E.C. Waters—just like the lake water—got the idea to sell boat trips to the public on Yellowstone Lake. Ever since then, people who want to take a ride can pay to do so. These days,

E. C. Waters's boat Zillah carried 125 people at a time on tours of Yellowstone Lake.

trips take an hour.

While always a very popular recreational opportunity, fishing on Yellowstone Lake has become more complicated. In 1994, it was learned lake trout, a much bigger kind of trout, was living in Yellowstone Lake and eating all of the cutthroat trout. This was a surprise because lake trout had never lived in the lake before, which that meant somebody illegally put them in.

The lake trout could put an end to a long-time tradition. Visitors wanted the cutthroat trout to continue on as the most important fish in the lake, but it was being threatened. The cutthroat trout also played a big part in the health of the environment and the animals who counted on them as part of their diet.

At great cost, for years now, a program has been in place to remove millions of lake trout from the lake. Millions of dollars have been spent, but the plan is working. The cutthroat trout are slowly taking their old home back. Anyone who fishes on Yellowstone Lake now must take certain steps when they catch a fish. They have to release a cutthroat trout back into the water, and they must keep a lake trout and kill it.

The other kind of fishing in Yellowstone National Park, a sport people by the thousands come to participate in, is fly fishing. This is practiced on the rivers, sometimes standing on the shore, but often by standing in the water itself while wearing high rubber boots to stay dry. These fishermen use human-made flies as their lures (in place of real insects) to fool trout into biting their hooks. They must also release cutthroat trout back to the waters where they

Flyfishers in Yellowstone are only allowed to wade in while fishing, not fish from a boat.

caught them.

Chapter 12
What's Next

The National Park Service has the challenging job of managing Yellowstone so that it will be there for future generations. However, much of Yellowstone's preservation depends on the visitors. People can affect the Park in many ways, both directly and indirectly.

The Old Faithful Visitor Education Center educates guests on Yellowstone's history, volcanism, wildlife, and geothermal activity.

Sometimes, people think they are helping when they bring a lonely bison, deer, or goat into a ranger station. This is a way that people directly affect the Park. Most of the time the well-intentioned visitors don't think that they could actually be hurting the animal. Removing an animal from its natural habitat, especially a baby, is extremely dangerous, though. The person could get hurt by a scared animal or its mother. The baby could get separated and not be able to rejoin its herd or family. Animals are really better off where they are, without human interference.

If a visitor does see something that concerns them, they should report it to a ranger. The rangers are trained in the best way to help the animals. They will know whether they need to go get the animal, or leave it alone.

Climate change is also affecting Yellowstone National Park. On average, the temperature at Yellowstone has increased about 1/3 degree per decade. While that doesn't seem like a lot, over time it can add up. Increased water temperature affects Yellowstone's cutthroat trout, which is a food source for many animals in the Park. Also, animals who rely on the snow, like lynx and wolverines, will be in danger if snowfall continues to get lighter from winter to winter.

Yellowstone is considered fire-adapted, meaning controlled fires can be a good thing. Uncontrolled fires are dangerous, though.

With warmer summers, forest fires are more of a threat as brush and trees dry out from the heat. Fires are more common and spread quicker now than they did before. If fires start happening more frequently, as some scientists fear, the mountain forests could be affected. The forests have adapted to occasional forest fires, but if they happen too often, the trees won't have time to heal. This would change much of Yellowstone's mountainous areas from forest to field and woodland.

More volcanic activity could increase the temperature in Yellowstone as well. There is a popular myth that says that the supervolcano underneath Yellowstone caldera is overdue for a supereruption. This has been the subject of many fiction books and movies. Fortunately, it's just not true.

While scientists cannot say for sure when Yellowstone will erupt again, they do know that it won't be soon. Based on the timing of the last three supereruptions, Yellowstone shouldn't be ready to erupt for almost another million years. Yellowstone would warn scientists and geologists before an eruption through earthquakes. Some small earthquakes are normal at the Park and signal geyser eruptions or other geothermal activity. Big earthquakes are not normal and would mean something else is happening.

Yellowstone is much more likely to have smaller, less catastrophic eruptions. The past fifty eruptions have been simple lava flows, where molten rock breaks through the Earth's crust without an explosion. This happened in

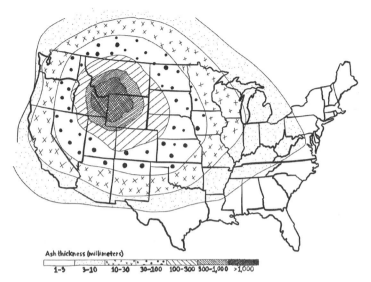

Ash thickness (millimeters)

| 1-5 | 5-10 | 10-30 | 30-100 | 100-300 | 300-1,000 | >1,000 |

If Yellowstone's supervolcano were to erupt,
the ash would affect places as far away as the east coast.

Iceland in 2018. While still able to cause harm, lava flows are the least dangerous of all the types of volcanic eruptions.

Another likely possibility is a geothermal eruption. This is similar to a geyser erupting, except larger and more explosive. A geothermal eruption happens when water trapped underground boils and builds up enough pressure to break through the ground above it. This eruption throws rock into the sky and can create a crater.

Visitors at Yellowstone don't have to worry about any of this, though. Yellowstone Volcano Observatory officials watch all of the activity in Yellowstone very carefully. They are dedicated to learning about Yellowstone's geothermal activity and making sure everyone is safe.

The creation of the National Park Service led to what is now more than 400 areas and 84 million acres reserved as national parks, momuments, or historical sites.

In 2022, Yellowstone National Park will be 150 years old. 2016 was the Park's busiest year on record, with over four million people venturing out to see the park. Park officials are hoping to beat that record in 2022. They anticipate many people traveling west to celebrate a century and half of the United States' best idea.

Select Quotes about Yellowstone

"All citizens of America, whether they realize it or not, are stewards of Yellowstone."

—Dan Wenk, former National Park Service superintendent of Yellowstone National Park.

"I think the principle of having the parks free is the proper one and we hope that the time will come when we can make them free to motorists as well as others."

—Stephen Mather, first director of the National Park Service.

"One day during this era [1960s] I counted seven different grizzlies and five different black bears in the Canyon Campground over a four-hour span of time [afternoon to dark]. If this were to happen today, it would make the front page of most major newspapers."

—Jerry Mernin, former Yellowstone National Park ranger.

"The Yellowstone idea is a generous one, and a patriotic one. It requires us to save for common purposes, for everybody, some of this land. And not just a little bit of wonder here and another bit there."

—Roger Kennedy, former director of the National Park Service.

"In God's wildness lies the hope of the world—the great, fresh, unblighted wilderness."

—Naturalist John Muir

Yellowstone Timeline

1808   After participating in the Lewis and Clark Expedition, mountain man John Colter sets out on his own in the wild territory of the Yellowstone. He reports seeing steam, boiling water, the earth on fire. Only no one believes him.

1860   The first organized expedition of Yellowstone Plateau is attempted but fails.

1870   The Henry Washburn Expedition documents many geysers and names Old Faithful because it regularly erupts (at that time) every hour.

1871   An expedition led by Ferdinand Vandeveer Hayden expands Yellowstone exploration. Photographs taken by William Henry Jackson and paintings made by artist Thomas Moran are displayed in Washington, D.C. and excite those who see them.

1872   Congress passes legislation establishing Yellowstone as the first National Park in the world and President Ulysses S. Grant signs it into law.

1872   Nathaniel P. Langford, who traveled with Henry Washburn's group, is named the first superintendent of Yellowstone.

1880-1881   Harry Yount is hired as gamekeeper for Yellowstone – the first Park Ranger. His job is to patrol the Park and discourage lawbreakers from killing animals.

1886   The U.S. Army takes over operations in Yellowstone National Park.

1891   The Clean Air Act Amendments requires Yellowstone to start monitoring air quality to ensure that requirements of the act are being met.

World Timeline

1804 Alexander Hamilton and Aaron Burr have their infamous duel mortally wounding Hamilton.

1864 Yosemite becomes the first park to be protected by the government, but it is supervised by the state of California. Yosemite becomes a National Park in 1890.

1871 Chicago fire results in 250 deaths.

1872 Jules Verne releases his book Around the World in Eighty Days, one of the most famous books of all time.

1875 1st Kentucky Derby is held at Churchill Downs, originally called the Louisville Jockey Club Course.

1876 In what is regarded as the last gasp of Native Americans to save their lands, Gen. George Armstrong Custer's 7th Cavalry is wiped out at the Battle of the Little Bighorn.

1879 Thomas Edison invents the first practical form of electric light.

1885 The first skyscraper in the world is finished in Chicago.

1890 In an influential essay, historian Frederick Jackson Turner famously declares the American frontier closed.

Yellowstone Timeline (cont.)

1904   Some 13,927 people visit Yellowstone National Park.

1915   The first cars are officially allowed into Yellowstone National Park

1916   The Army withdraws from administration of Yellowstone.

1933-1942   The Civilian Conservation Corps, created by President Franklin D. Roosevelt to provide jobs during the Great Depression, builds facilities in Yellowstone.

1943   Attributed to World War II, attendance plummets to 61,696, a drop of more than 500,000 since 1941.

1948   For the first time more than 1 million people visit Yellowstone in one year.

1963   The Leopold Report, officially known as Wildlife Management in the National Parks, is released. This begins a new, modern management of Yellowstone and other national parks.

1966   A new thermophile called Thermus aquaticus is discovered in a Yellowstone hot spring.

1970   Rules are implemented ending the daily feeding of garbage to bears in Yellowstone.

1972   The number of grizzly bears in the Yellowstone area declines to 136 and the animal given federal protection under the Endangered Species Act.

1972   The 100th anniversary of the creation of Yellowstone is celebrated.

World Timeline (cont.)

1900   Congress passes the Lacey Act, which provides criminal penalties for those illegally taking game, fish or plant life and attempting to profit from it.

1914-1918   World War I

1916   The National Park Service is created to supervise all of the country's National Parks.

1930   Pluto is discovered by astronomers.

1941-1945   United States participates in World War II.

1948   Gandhi is assassinated in New Delhi.

1963   President John F. Kennedy is assassinated.

1964   United States passes the Civil Rights Act.

1968   Civil Rights leader Martin Luther King Jr. assassinated.

1969   American Neil Armstrong walks on the moon.

1974   President Richard Nixon resigns because of the Watergate Scandal.

1989   Berlin Wall separating east and west comes down in Germany.

1994   Nelson Mandela becomes first black president of South Africa.

Yellowstone Timeline (cont.)

1988   Forest fires burn more than 793,000 square miles, one-third of the Park, of Yellowstone, over the summer.

1995   Wolves are restored to Yellowstone Park.

2002   The National Academy of Science confirms the effectiveness of Ecological Process Management, a.k.a. natural regulation.

2016   Yellowstone sets a one-year record of 4.2 million visitors.

2017   Claiming the Yellowstone grizzly bear has recovered as a species and its population grown to about 700, the U.S. Fish and Wildlife Service delists it from Endangered Species Act protection.

World Timeline (cont.)

2001   iPhone introduced, triggering new cell phone revolution.

2001   World Trade Center in New York destroyed by terrorists.

2008   Barack Obama elected first African-American president in American history.

2016   Businessman Donald Trump elected 45th president of the United States, highlighting deep political divisions within country.

Glossary

Bears   There are two kinds of bears in Yellowstone National Park. Grizzly bears are the biggest ones and usually have brown fur. Black bears are smaller and usually have black fur. There are many fewer grizzly bears in the United States than black bears and they are much harder to see in the wilderness.

Bison/Buffalo   When they are talking, Americans usually describe this animal as buffalo, but the official scientific name is bison. These animals do not look like any other kind of animals in Yellowstone National Park. They are larger than all of the others, sometimes weighing 2000 pounds, with huge heads, furry brown coats, and travel in herds, sometimes more than one hundred of them together.

Cutthroat Trout   A kind of fish that were always in Yellowstone National Park. They are considered very beautiful because of the colors on their bodies, but over the years the number of them has gone down because too many people fished for them and other kinds of fish began eating them.

Endangered Species Act   A law passed in 1973 that is intended to protect everything—mammals, fish, birds, plants, and insects—if they are in danger of extinction.

Forest Fires   Most of the time when a fire breaks out and begins to burn down trees, it is located deep in the woods or forest and is started by lighting bolts. Sometimes, though, careless people start fires because they do not put out their camp fires all the way. Forest fires can be very dangerous to visitors and the animals that live in the woods. They can also be good for the land in helping to start new growth.

Geothermal Features   The geysers and hot springs inside Yellowstone National Park which either send boiling water high into the sky because of activity below the ground, or which produce steam from standing pools of water.

Grand Prismatic Spring   There are many hot springs in Yellowstone, but this is the most famous one. It stands out because the water has the most colors. Its water often looks much brighter than the regular blue of water in oceans.

Gray Wolf   This kind of wolf is in the canine family, where dogs come from, but the wolf lives in the wild and is bigger than most kinds of dogs. There was a time when Yellowstone National Park officials did not want any wolves left in the park and got rid of them. Much later, they brought them back to their old home ranges.

Junior Rangers   Usually kids who are between five and 13 years old. They can earn badges by finishing tasks, can obtain booklets about the National Parks written for children and can get passports that are stamped when they visit National Parks.

Mountain Men   In the early days of the United States, before states were created west of the Mississippi River, rugged men dressed in furs and buckskins hunted and trapped in wild country to make their living off the land.

National Park   One of 59 beautiful places in the United States the federal government has set aside to protect for all time so future generations of Americans can enjoy their scenery, whether it is mountains, canyons, rivers, or seashores.

National Park Service   A federal government agency that supervises all of the United States's national parks to make sure everything runs smoothly.

Native Americans   The first people who lived in this country thousands of years before it became the United States. They are often called Indians.

Old Faithful   This is the most famous geyser in the world and is a very popular place for visitors to Yellowstone National Park. The geyser received its name in the 19th century because it erupts on a regular pattern all day long and through the night, these days about once every 75 minutes, each time sending hot water 100 feet into the sky.

Park Rangers   The uniformed men and women who help protect animals that live in national parks. They enforce the rules so visitors can stay safe.

Poaching   When hunters illegally kill animals.

Sierra Club   This is an organization with its headquarters in California that was founded in 1892 with the goal of keeping the United States' environment healthy and protecting wild creatures.

Superintendent   The boss of all the workers and happenings inside each national park.

Supervolcano   Volcanos exist deep in the earth below Yellowstone National Park, although there has been no eruption for thousands and thousands of years. Scientists predict that some day – far in the future – a big eruption will take place caused by what is called a Super Volcano.

Tourists   The people who come from all over to visit a place.

Yellowstone National Park   The 2.2-millon-acre park which stretches into parts of Wyoming, Montana, and Idaho that was established as the world's first national park in 1872.

Bibliography

Sources

Oh, Ranger! by Horace M. Albright and Frank Taylor.

Summer of Fire by Jim Carrier.

The Birth of the National Park Service, The Founding Years, 1913-1933, by Horace M. Albright and Robert Cahn.

The Discovery of Yellowstone Park by Nathaniel P. Langford.

Wrecked In Yellowstone by Mike Stark

Yellowstone: 125 Years of America's Best Idea by Michael Milstein.

Further Reading

59 Illustrated National Parks, 100th Anniversary of the National Park Service, Joel Anderson and Nathan Anderson.

Adventures In Yellowstone: Early Travelers Tell Their Tales by M. Mark Miller.

The National Parks: America's Best Idea by Dayton Duncan and Ken Burns.

The Stories Of Yellowstone: Adventure Tales From The World's First National Park by M. Mark Miller.

YELLOWSTONE: A Journey Through America's Wild Heart by David Quammen.

Yellowstone Ranger by Jerry Mernin

Index

Index (cont.)

Index (cont.)

Index (cont.)

Index (cont.)

Index (cont.)